Earn Wisely

BY HEATHER E. SCHWARTZ

amicus high interest

Amicus High Interest is published by Amicus
P.O. Box 1329, Mankato, MN 56002
www.amicuspublishing.us

Library of Congress Cataloging-in-Publication Data
Schwartz, Heather E.
 Earn wisely / Heather E. Schwartz.
     pages cm. – (Money smarts)
Includes bibliographical references and index.
Audience: K to Grade 3.
ISBN 978-1-60753-793-9 (library binding)
ISBN 978-1-60753-902-5 (ebook)
1. Money-making projects for children–Juvenile literature.
2. Entrepreneurship–Juvenile literature. 3. Money–Juvenile
literature. I. Title.
 HF5392.S37 2016
 650.1–dc23
                              2014033281

Editor: Wendy Dieker
Series Designer: Kathleen Petelinsek
Book Designer: Aubrey Harper
Photo Researcher: Derek Brown

Photo Credits: Jonathan Gelber/fstop/Corbis cover; Tetra
Images/Corbis 5; JGI/Jamie Grill/Blend Images/Corbis 6;
Radius Images/Corbis 9; Tanya Constantine/Blend Images/
Corbis 10; Tetra Images/Corbis 12-13; Tetra Images/Corbis
14; KidStock/Blend Images/Corbis 17; Inti St Clair/Getty
18; Tetra Images/Corbis 21; 2/Ocean/Corbis 22-23; Tim
Pannell/Corbis 25; KidStock/Blend Images/Corbis 26; 68/
Compassionate Eye Foundation/Ocean/Corbis 29

Printed in Malaysia.

10 9 8 7 6 5 4 3 2 1

Table of Contents

Making Your Own Money   **4**

Sold!   **8**

Getting the Job Done   16

Earning More   24

You've Earned It!   **28**

Glossary   30

Read More   **31**

Websites   31

Index   **32**

Making Your Own Money

If you're like most kids, there's something
you want. Maybe it's a new computer
game. Maybe it's a pair of shoes. Whatever
you want, you need money to buy it.
But, as the old saying goes, money doesn't
grow on trees. That means money isn't
easy to get. You have to work to get
money. You have to earn it.

Earning money can be hard work, but it's worth it in the end.

Kids can find plenty of small jobs to earn money.

 Can kids get hired to work at places like grown-ups?

Many adults you know probably have jobs. They get paid to do their jobs. Kids can earn money, too. They can sell things they own. They can sell things they make. They can even provide **services** for other people. Kids can do chores at home or for others to earn some money.

 Not until they are 14. Younger kids can deliver newspapers or help with family businesses.

Sold!

Do you have toys and games you don't want? You can earn money by selling them. Have a yard sale. First, talk to your parents about a sale. Then, sort your items. Put a price tag on each item, or make signs listing prices. Put signs up around your neighborhood. The signs should let people know when and where your sale is.

Garage sales help you get rid of clutter and even earn some money.

This girl earned money selling a dollhouse she doesn't want anymore.

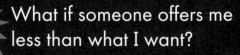

Q What if someone offers me less than what I want?

How do you know what price to put on your things? Let's say you have a toy car to sell. See how much a new one costs. Because yours is used, your price should be less than the new price. If your toy still looks new, you could ask half of the new price. If it is worn out, people won't pay very much for it. Put a lower price on it.

 This is called **haggling**. You can decide! If you really want to sell your item, you can sell it for less. Or you can wait for another buyer.

You can also earn money
by making things to sell.
Can you make lemonade?
Open a lemonade stand.
You'll need a pitcher of
lemonade, cups, and a table.
Make a sign to tell the price
per cup. Be sure to set up
your stand in a busy place so
people find you.

A lemonade stand is a
fun way to earn money.

Lemonade

Give customers a good price, but don't lose money by charging too little.

Q I want to make money faster. Can I charge $10 for a cup of lemonade?

What about pricing on things you make? Let's say you spend $8 on lemonade supplies. If you make 40 cups, each cup will **cost** you 20 cents. You will have to charge more than that to make money. If you sell each cup for 75 cents, you will earn 55 cents per cup.

Sure! But people don't like to pay too much for things. They probably will buy lemonade from someone who sells it for less money.

Getting the Job Done

Maybe you don't have things to sell. Don't worry. You can also earn money by providing services. Chores you do at home are services. You could set the table. You could feed the cat. You could dust the furniture. When you're paid for chores at home, you earn an **allowance**.

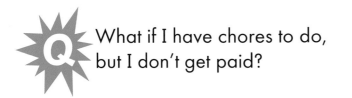

What if I have chores to do, but I don't get paid?

Setting the table is a good service job you can do to earn money.

A Some parents don't pay for jobs that help the whole family. Ask your parents if they will pay you for doing extra chores.

Babysitting can be a good way to earn money.

Q What if I don't feel safe at someone's house?

You can also work for your neighbors. Ask if they'll pay for your help. Do you like to do yard work? Offer to sweep the sidewalk or rake leaves. Do you like young kids? You can play with them so a parent can get some work done.

 You should leave. Always be sure your parents know where you are. Tell your parents if you don't feel safe doing a job.

So how much should you get paid to work? Find out what other kids get paid for that job. You can charge about the same price. Remember that not all jobs are the same. You can ask for more money for a hard job. Easy jobs should be cheaper.

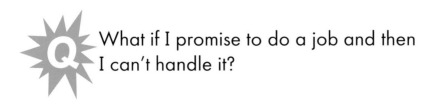

What if I promise to do a job and then I can't handle it?

**If you want to make money,
offer a fair price for your work.**

 If you can't get the job done, apologize.
Offer to give up some or all of your pay.

To get jobs, you have to **advertise**. Tell people what jobs you can do. Print **flyers** to hand out. List your job and your phone number. Ask your parents if you can post the flyers in your neighborhood. Don't forget to tell people in person too!

Hang up signs to let people know what job you will do.

Earning More

Now you've found a job you like. How can you keep earning more? Ask your customers to **refer** you if you do a good job. That means they tell their friends about you. It is a good way to get new customers.

Take time to do a good job. People will tell their friends to hire you.

If you do your best work, you
might get a little extra money.

When you do jobs for people or sell something, do your best. You might earn a **tip**. A tip is when someone pays you a little more than your price. People pay tips when they think you worked extra hard or you gave them good service. You shouldn't ask for a tip. But if you get one, say, "Thank you."

You've Earned It!

Earning money isn't always easy. Selling things is work. Doing jobs for others is work, too. Work can be hard. But it can be fun, too. You might like some jobs more than others. You can choose to do jobs you know you'll enjoy. Soon you will have your own money. What will you spend it on?

Sweeping sidewalks can be hard work. But the money earned can be worth it!

Glossary

advertise To tell people about your sale or service; making signs is one way to advertise.

allowance Money kids get from their parents; some kids get money for doing chores, but others get it for being part of the family.

cost The amount of money you need to spend to sell things; you need to buy cups and lemonade to sell lemonade.

flyers Sheets of paper that list information about services or things for sale.

haggling When the buyer and seller try to agree on a different price for something for sale.

refer To tell someone about a good experience they had when buying something or receiving someone's services.

services Jobs you do to help people, like washing dishes or yard work.

tip A bit of extra money that buyers give if they think the service or product was extra good.

Read More

Heos, Bridget. *Make Money! Do Yard Work.* Mankato, Minn.: Amicus, 2014.

Rissman, Rebecca. *Earning Money.* Chicago: Heinemann Library, 2008.

Scheunemann, Pam. *Cool Jobs for Kids Who Like Kids: Ways to Make Money Working with Children.* Minneapolis: ABDO Publishing Co, 2011.

Websites

KidzWorld: Quiz! What's Your Job Personality
www.kidzworld.com/quiz/2815-quiz-whats-your-job-personality

The Mint: Earning
www.themint.org/kids/earning.html

PBS Kids: It's My Life: Money
pbskids.org/itsmylife/money

Index

advertising 22
allowance 16
chores 7, 16
costs 11, 15
customers 24
flyers 22
getting paid 7, 16, 20
jobs 7, 20, 22, 24,
    27, 28
lemonade stand 12
money 4, 7, 8, 12, 15,
    16, 20, 28

neighbors 19
pricing 8, 11, 12, 15, 20
referrals 24
selling things 7, 8, 11,
    12, 15, 27, 28
services 7, 16
signs 8, 12
tips 27
yard sale 8
yard work 19

About the Author

Heather E. Schwartz has written books for young readers on all kinds of topics. She was excited to write about money because it can be earned and used in so many interesting ways. She recently spent some savings on a fun purchase: two kittens! Visit Heather's website at www.heathereschwartz.com.